HELP!
I NEED A MAID

BY ELIZA MARKARYAN

DORRANCE
PUBLISHING CO
EST. 1920
PITTSBURGH, PENNSYLVANIA 15238

The contents of this work, including, but not limited to, the accuracy of events, people, and places depicted; opinions expressed; permission to use previously published materials included; and any advice given or actions advocated are solely the responsibility of the author, who assumes all liability for said work and indemnifies the publisher against any claims stemming from publication of the work.

All Rights Reserved
Copyright © 2023 by Eliza Markaryan

No part of this book may be reproduced or transmitted, downloaded, distributed, reverse engineered, or stored in or introduced into any information storage and retrieval system, in any form or by any means, including photocopying and recording, whether electronic or mechanical, now known or hereinafter invented without permission in writing from the publisher.

Dorrance Publishing Co
585 Alpha Drive
Pittsburgh, PA 15238
Visit our website at *www.dorrancebookstore.com*

ISBN: 979-8-8852-7195-0
eISBN: 979-8-8852-7651-1

HELP!
I NEED A MAID

Hi, my name is Fred, I put in an ad for aid.

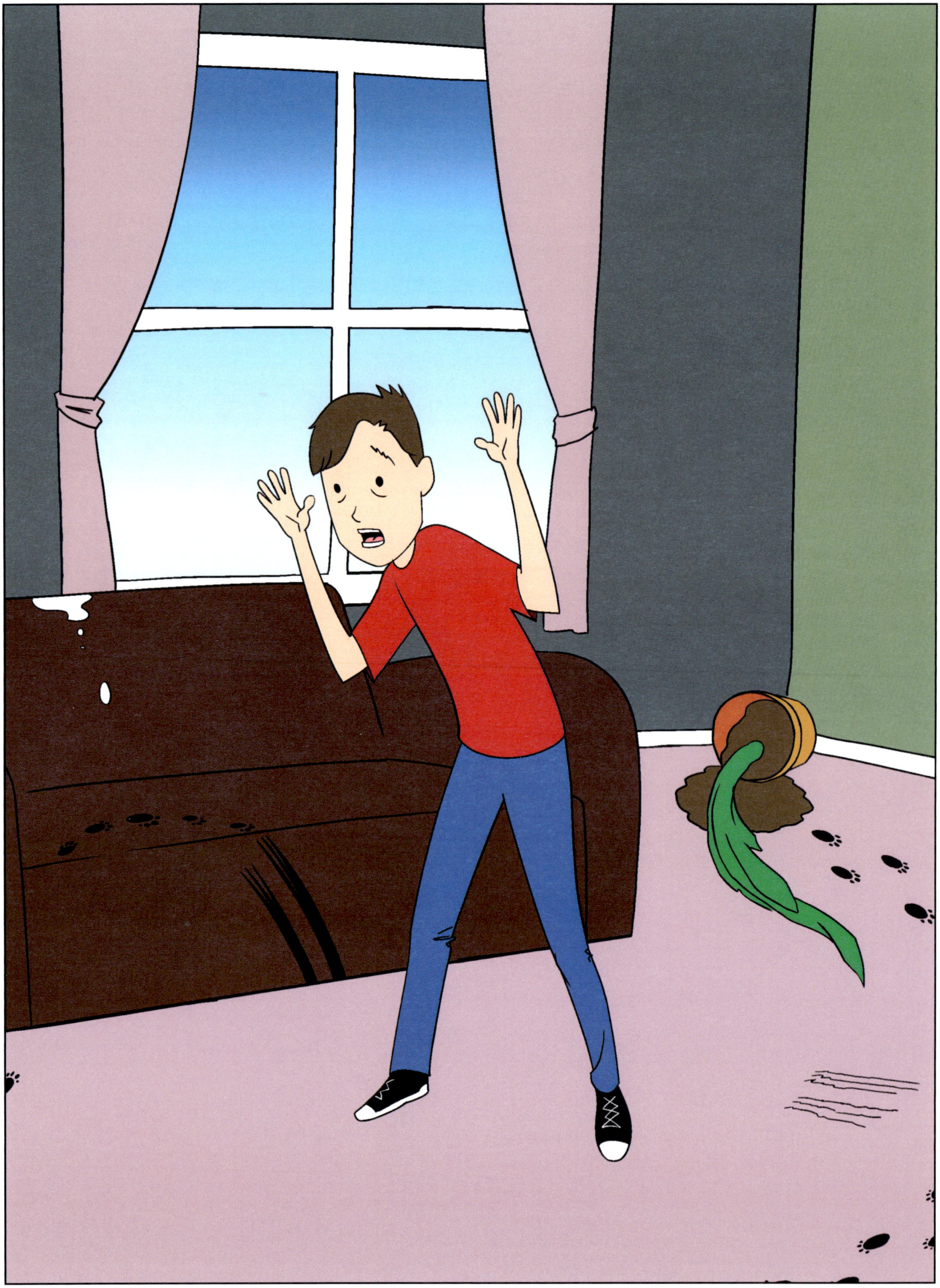

Oh boy, do I need an aid.

You heard me, that's what I said, I need a maid.

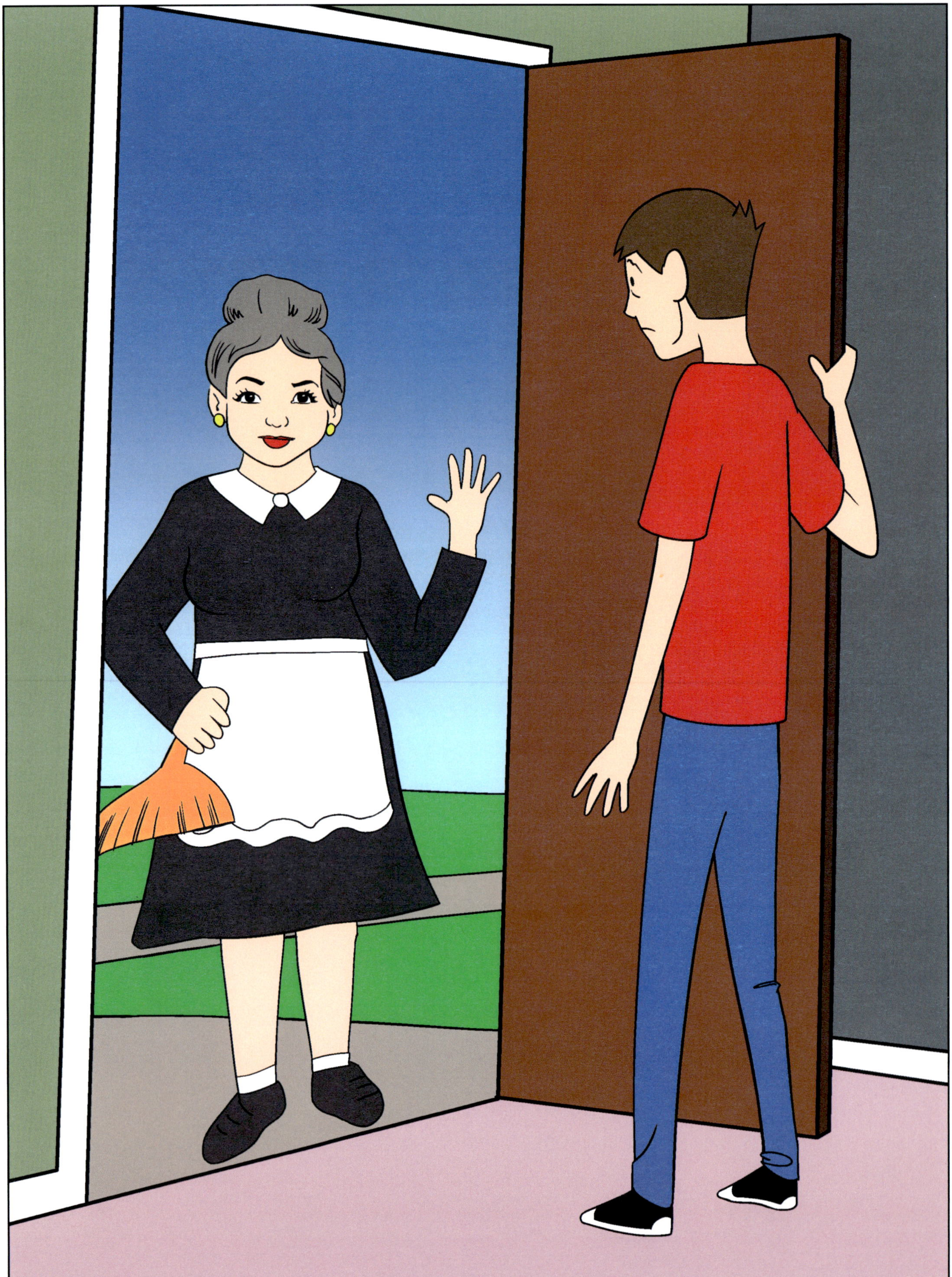

Knock! Knock! Who is there?

"It's Ms. Red. Your ad read that you need a maid for an aid."

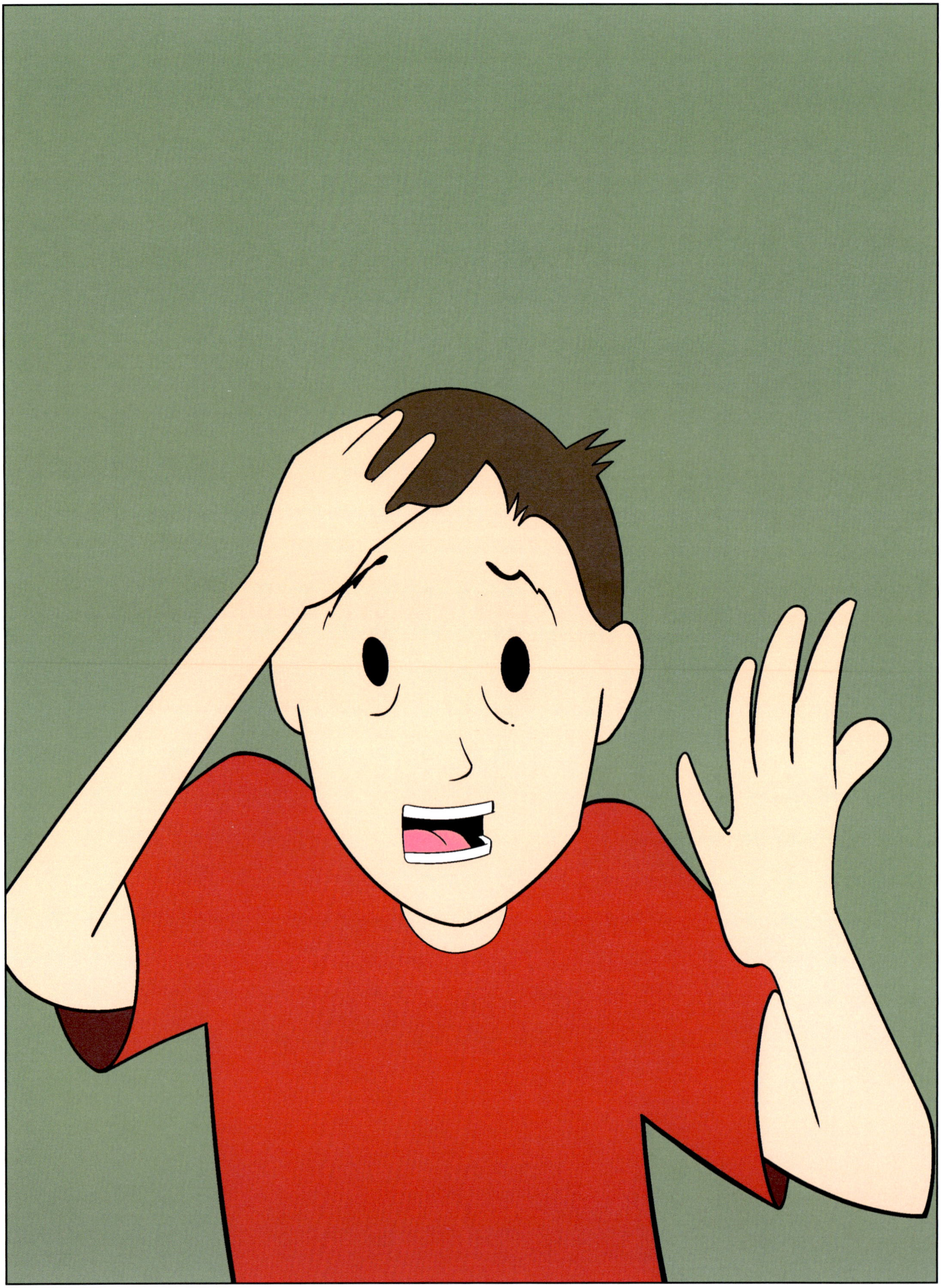

"Come in, Ms. Red. Tell me what you said. Are you here to give me an aid?

Will I finally have a maid?"

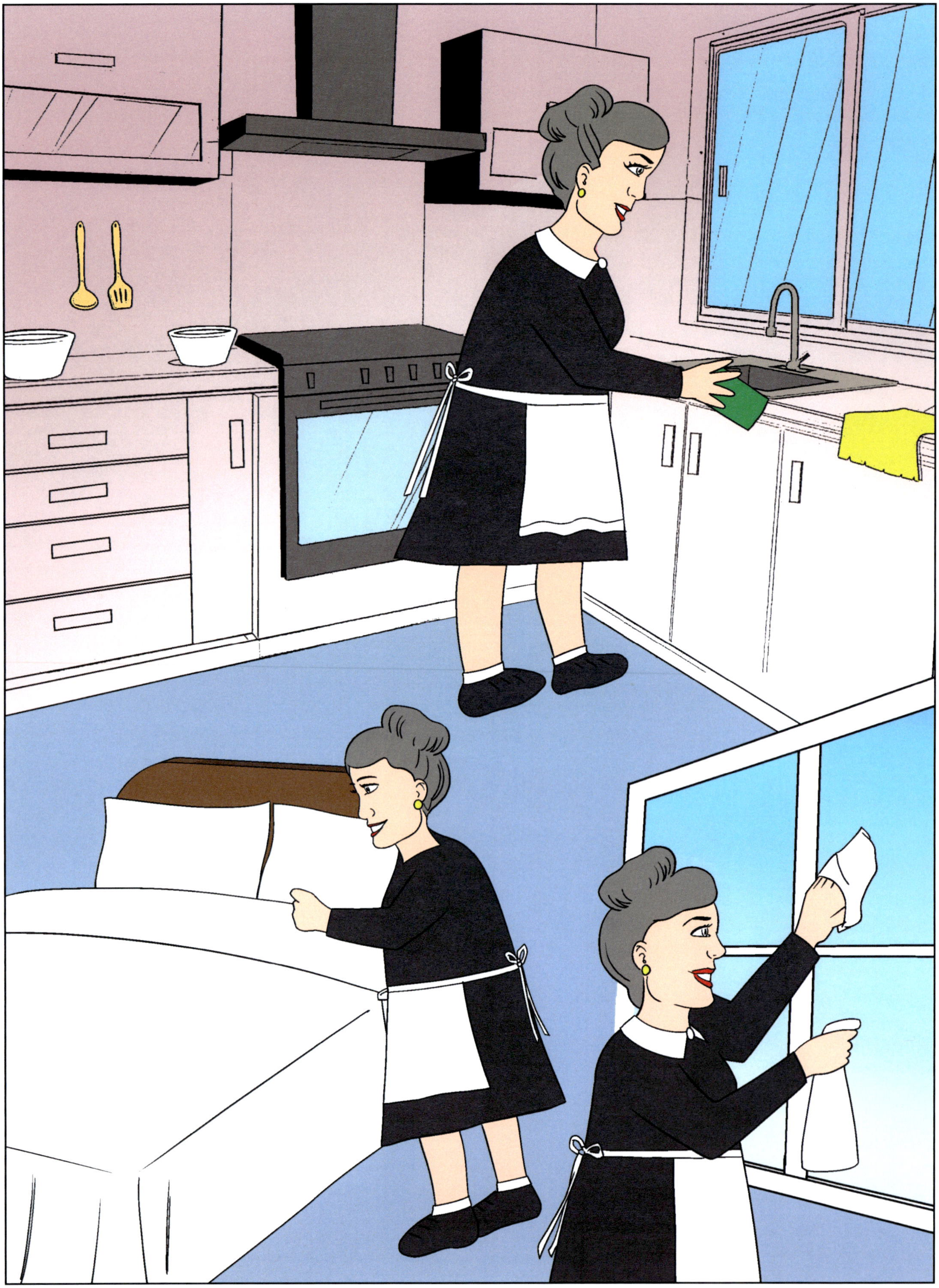

"Yes, I can cook, clean, and make your bed."

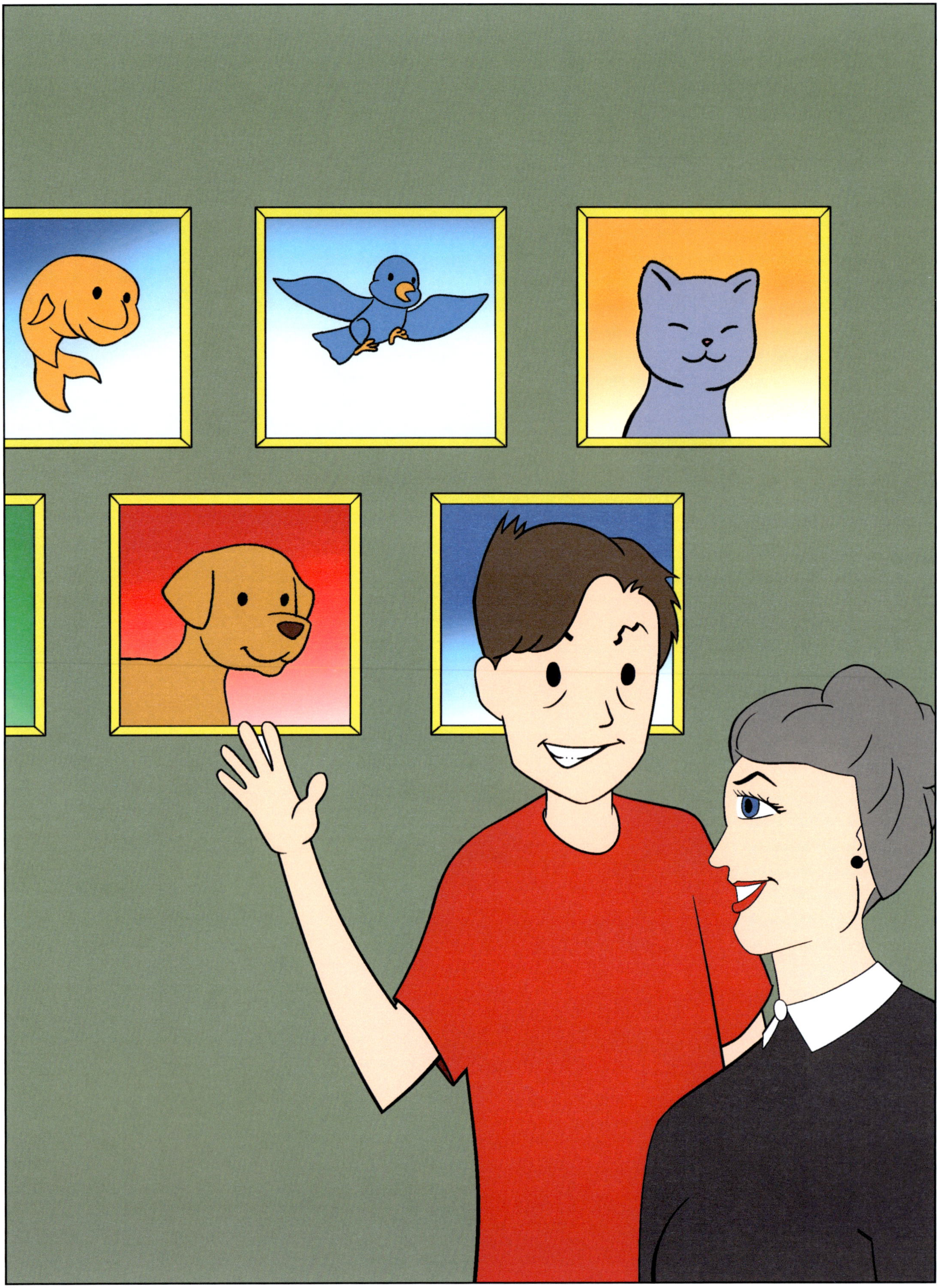

"Wow, then let me show you around, Ms. Red.

Here is Ed, my cat; Fred, my dog; Ned, my fish; Ted, my parakeet."

"Whoa, Mr. Fred, in the ad it did not say I give aid for four."

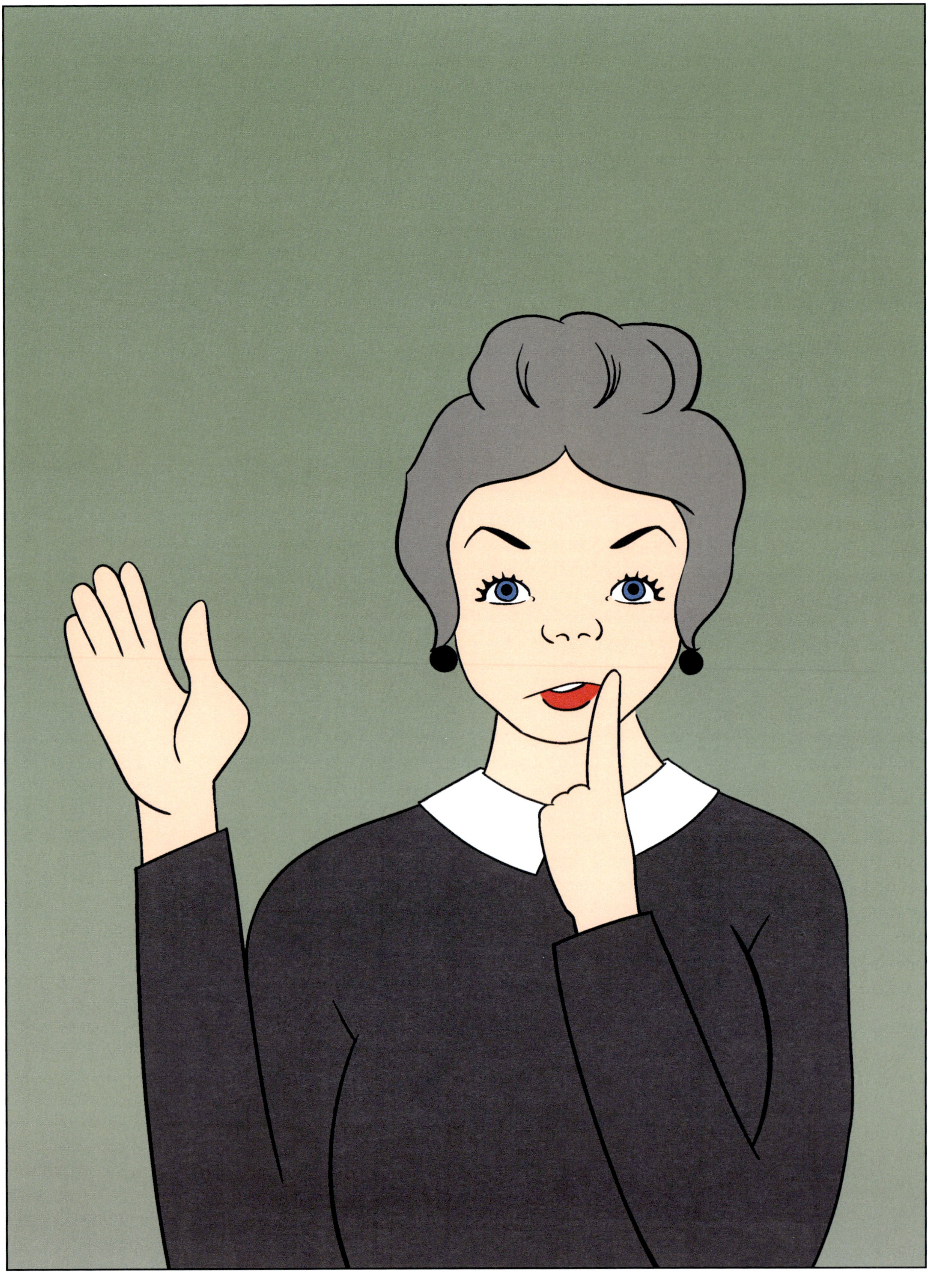

"Oh no, Ms. Red, that's not all. There is more."

"More, you said, Mr. Fred?"

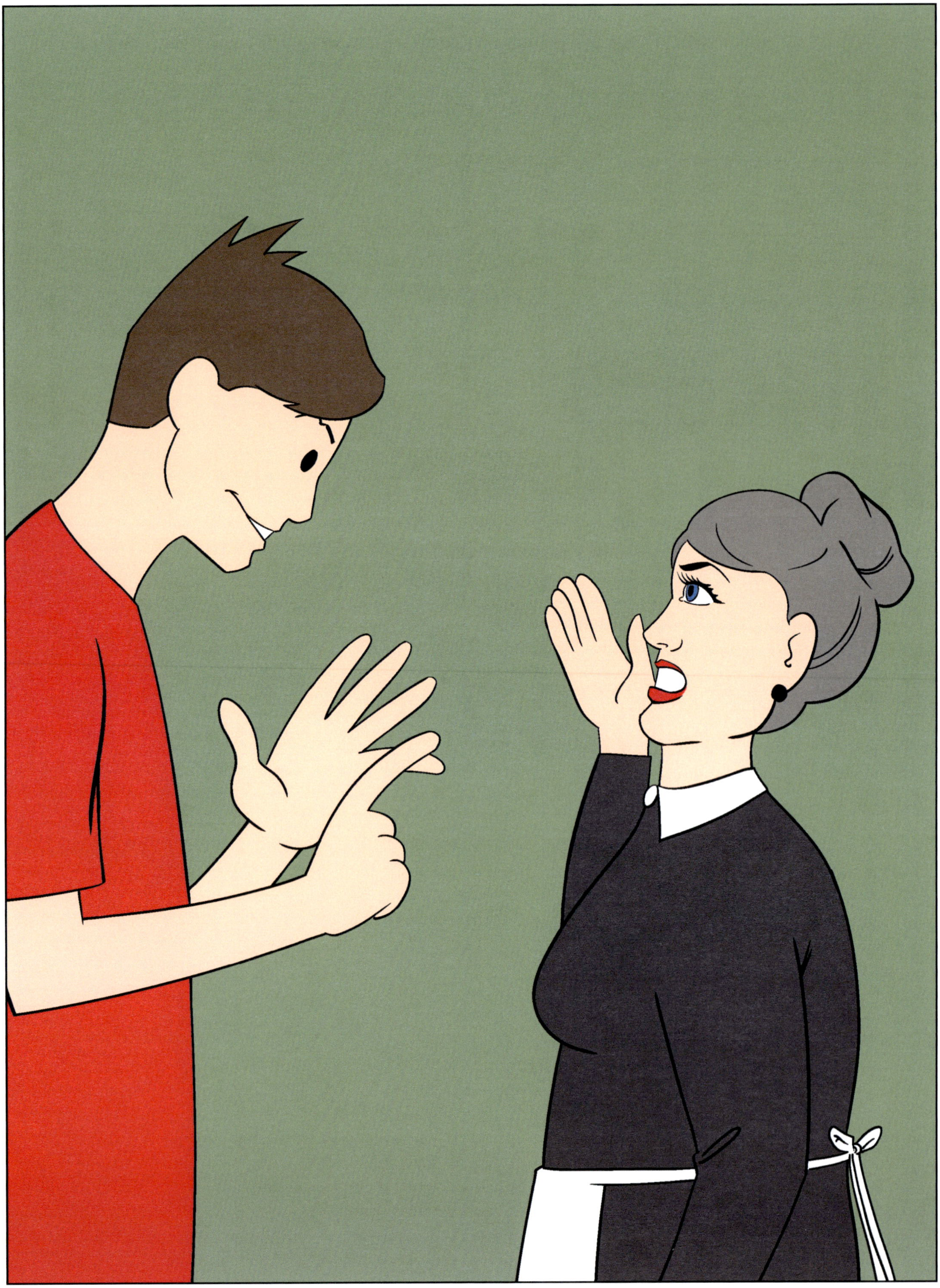

"Yes, there is my crocodile Zed, my snake Sled, my monkey Med, and my tiger Fed.

Ed, Fred, Ned, Ted, Zed, Sled, Med, and Fed all need to be walked, washed, fed, and put to bed."

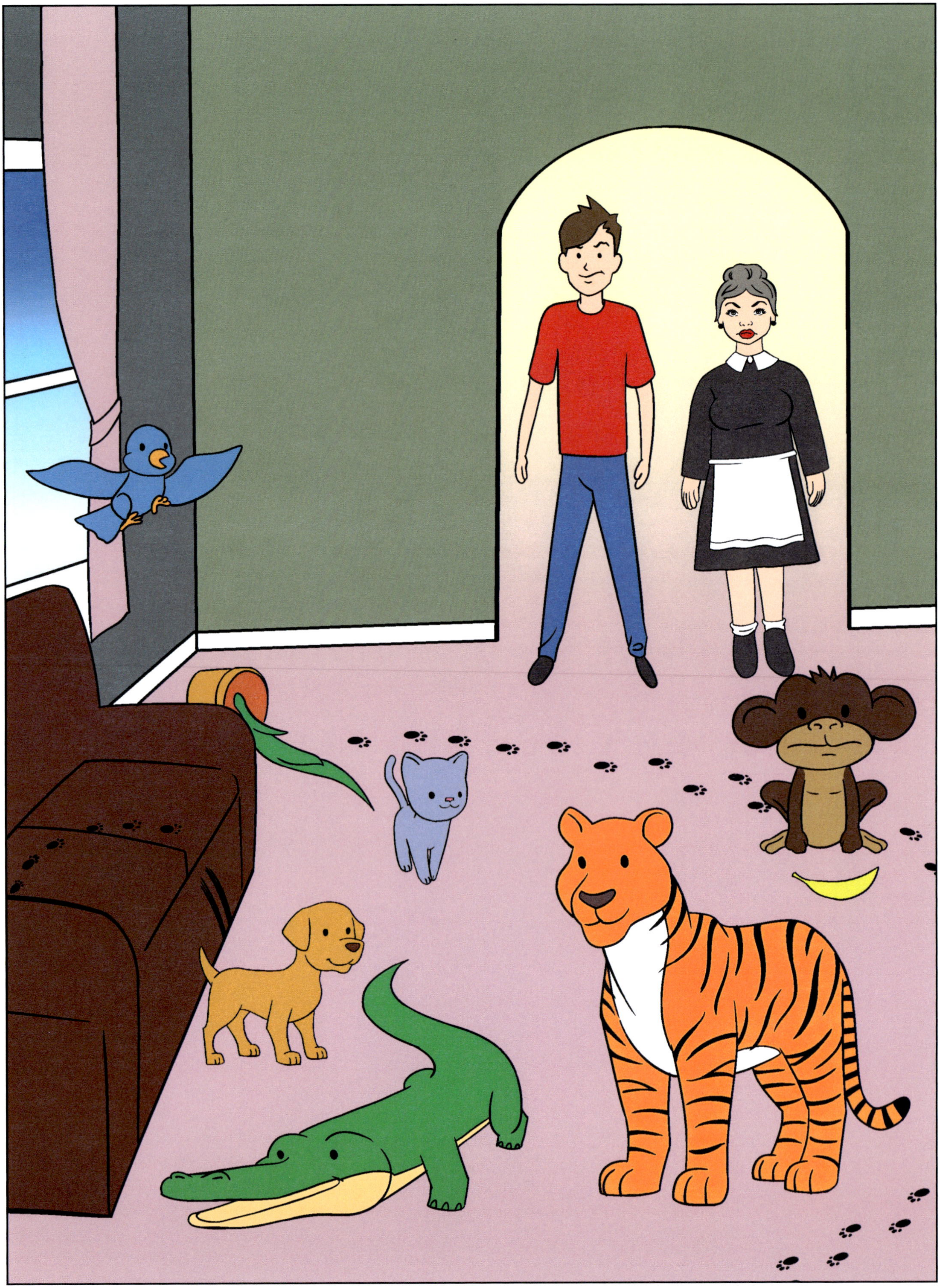

"Oh, Mr. Fred, I understand the cat, the dog, the fish, and the parakeet, but the crocodile, the snake, the monkey, and the tiger. No way, I say, Mr. Fred. What you need is not a maid. What you need is a zookeeper instead. So goodbye, Mr. Fred, and never call me again."

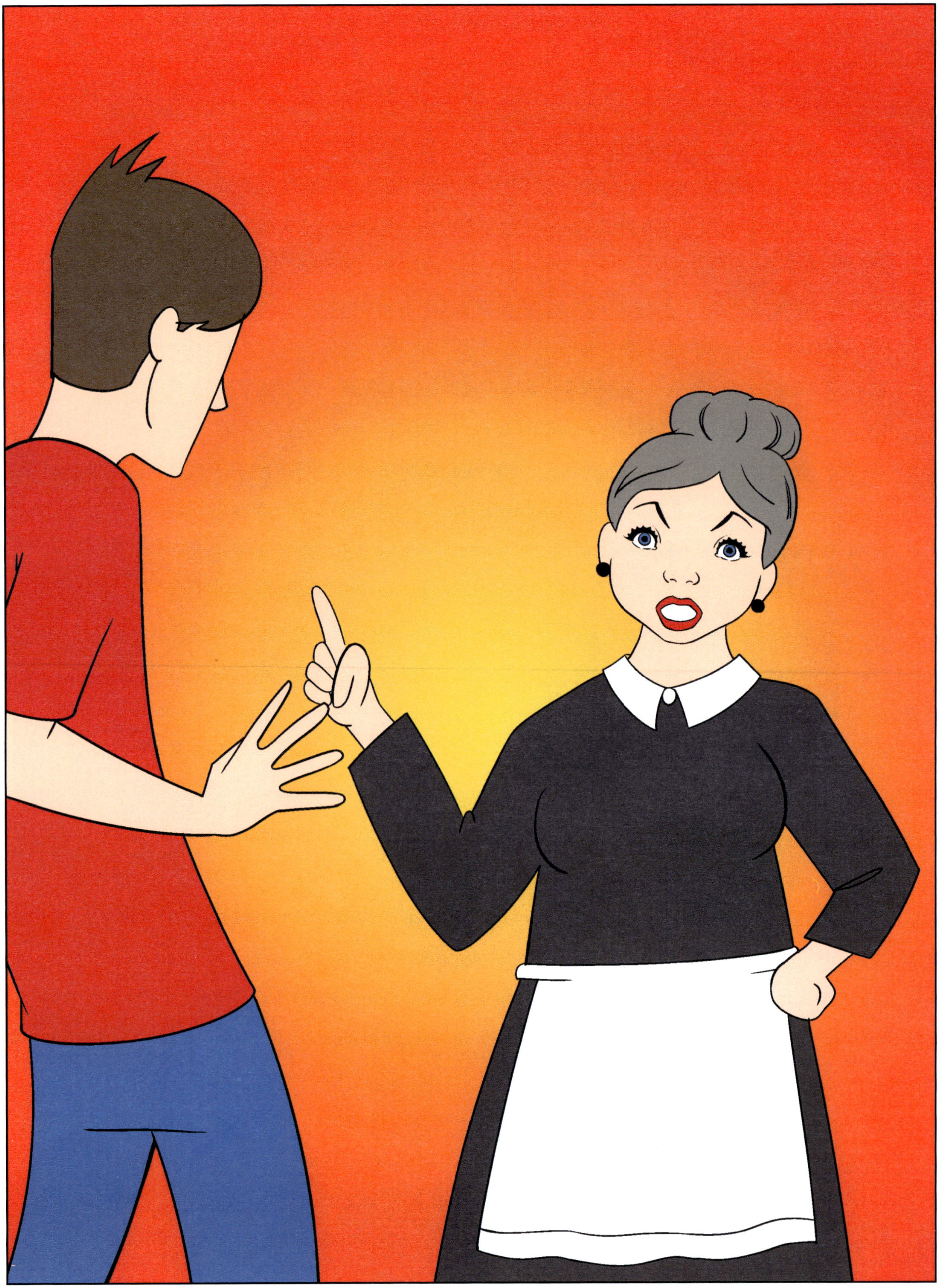

"Oh well, let me put out my ad again." *Looking For Maid Who Can Give Me Aid, 52nd attempt.*

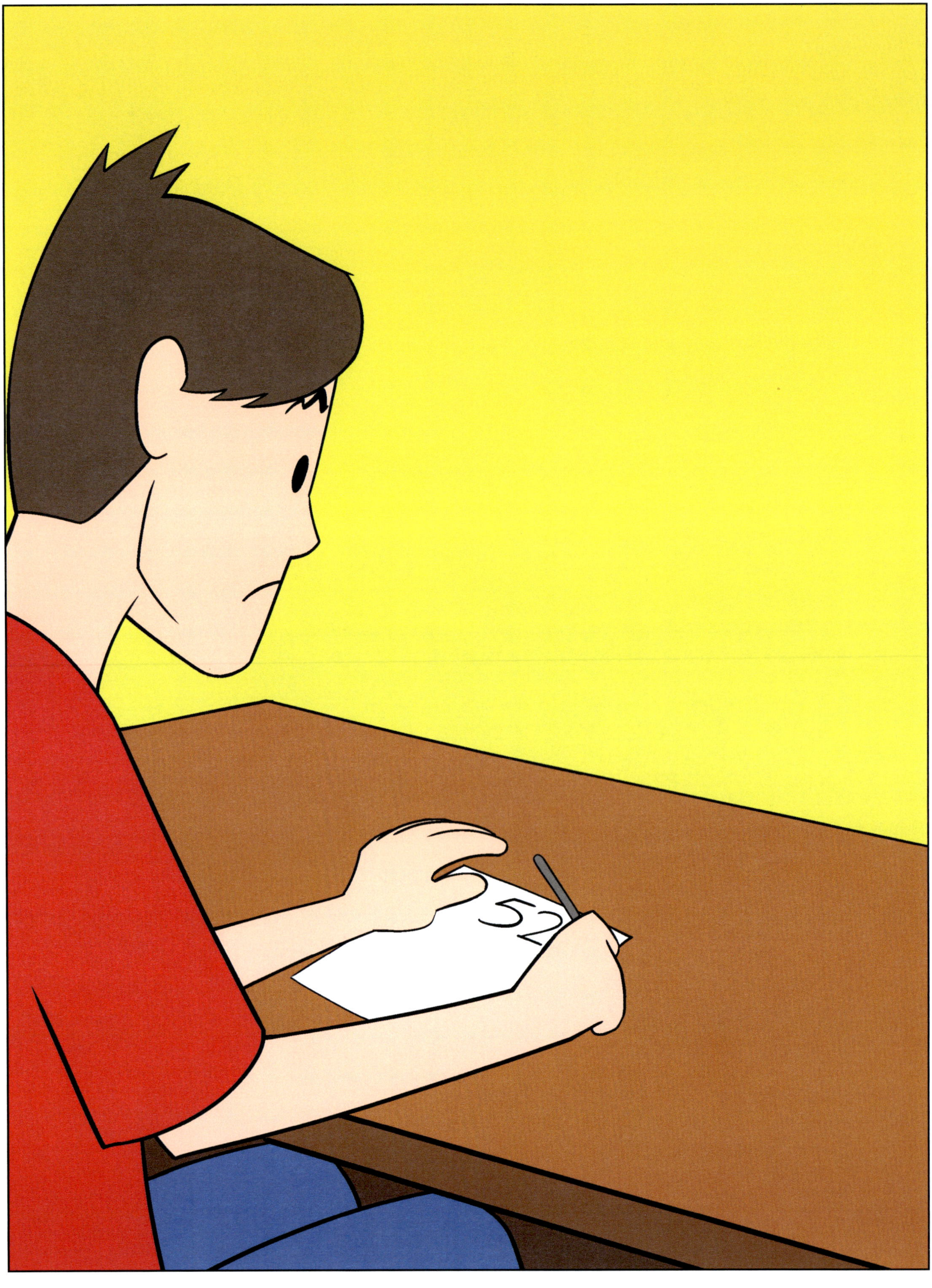
52

Will I ever find the right maid? I guess my friend who said finding a maid who gives you aid is not easy, so do not get that ahead.